AN ESSA ON MAN

D0143594

The Library of Liberal Arts

OSKAR PIEST, FOUNDER

AN ESSAY ON MAN

ALEXANDER POPE

Edited, with an Introduction, by

FRANK BRADY

The Library of Liberal Arts

published by
Macmillan Publishing Company
New York
Collier Macmillan Publishers
London

Alexander Pope: 1688-1744
An Essay on Man was originally published in 1733–1734

Macmillan Publishing Company
113 Sylvan Avenue, Englewood Cliffs, NJ 07632

First Edition

PRINTING   22 23 24 25 26 27 28   YEAR   9 0 1 2 3 4 5

Library of Congress Catalog Card Number: 65-26533
ISBN: 0-02-313460-7

CONTENTS

AN ESSAY ON MAN

INTRODUCTION

Alexander Pope is one of the most difficult of English poets, and for the modern reader the *Essay on Man* is perhaps the most remote of his works. To begin with, its very mode makes it suspect. In an age which seems to think that the ideal poem is a heavily metaphorical lyric, a didactic poem appears to be a contradiction in terms. Many a modern reader fresh from his first battle with the *Essay* would feel immediate sympathy with George II's supposed remark: "Who is this Pope that I hear so much about? I cannot discover what is his merit. Why will not my subjects write in prose?" We tend to assume that prose is the logical vehicle for thought, and poetry for emotion, though the slightest reflection indicates that an essay can express very strong feeling and that even the silliest poem tries to say something. And didactic poetry, though unpopular, continues to be written: W. H. Auden's *New Year Letter* takes its place in a long and honorable tradition which goes back to Lucretius' *On the Nature of Things* and Hesiod's *Works and Days*.

But even admitting the *Essay* is not a freak, the modern reader is likely to object to its high level of philosophical generalization, to ask if *this* poem would not read better, or at least more clearly, in prose. To this objection, Pope himself provides a partial answer in the "Design" prefixed to the poem: he chose verse because it is more memorable and more concise than prose. Behind these reasons lies a deeper one. Pope knew what many of his readers still forget: he was writing a didactic poem that presents a general "chain of reasoning" rather than a philosophic system. His poem was to be an *essay*, "an initial tentative effort," as *Webster's* defines the word: a sketch, not a rival to Aquinas' *Summa theologica*. To write in prose might well commit him to a rigorously technical argument for which he was not equipped and in which he was not interested. Pope wanted to demonstrate that the world made sense and in what ways it made sense, not as a philosopher but as an intelligent and educated layman. Or, as G. Wilson Knight puts the point: "We are watching something very rare: a poetic genius of the first order deliberately setting himself in maturity to create a compact and coherent system from his own creative centre."

Mr. Knight's last phrase might be misread. Pope shaped his materials creatively, but these materials were not spun out of himself: they were part of the common intellectual heritage of his time. He was not interested in being original; he was not exploring new worlds, but preparing "a general map" of the known world of human nature, since it was axiomatic that human nature was and always had been everywhere the same. What was needed was to discern its basic principles, to show man what he was, and consequently how he should think, feel, and act. Because man is a complex being, this was not easy; from the wild uproar of conflicting systems, each claiming to represent truth, Pope had to select and synthesize his materials. He was forced to steer "betwixt the extremes of doctrines seemingly opposite," and to do so through step-by-step argument could have been fatal.

The course Pope chose instead is illuminated by his own metaphor: he examined "the large, open, and perceptible parts" of "the anatomy of the mind," tracing connections, pointing out relationships, and showing that man's "nature and state" form part of a system as coherent as that of his body. As a result of this approach, the poem reveals not the logic of a Euclidean theorem but a series of complexly interwoven arguments, which present man from varying points of view as "glory, jest, and riddle." So in Epistle II, after this opening statement, Pope shows how pride in scientific knowledge acquired through reason makes man forget his lack of self-knowledge and self-control. Then, following the Epistle's central discussion of reason and passion, Pope closes (ll. 261 ff.) by showing how through the passions, fortified by hope and pride, man rests content in his little worlds of illusion. This passage balances the earlier discussion of scientific knowledge rather than following logically from it. As Martin Price remarks, the poem gives "more the effect of Metaphysical wit than versified argument; it is dialectical rather than didactic." The coherence of the *Essay* rests finally, to use Maynard Mack's phrase, "in inclusions, not conclusions."

Pope's lack of originality was Dr. Johnson's chief criticism of the poem: "Never were penury of knowledge and vulgarity of sentiment [commonplaceness of idea] so happily disguised. The reader feels his mind full, though he learns nothing; and when he meets it in its new array no longer knows the talk of his mother and his nurse." Ironically, this lack of originality is one of the poem's claims on the modern reader's attention; as well as any one work can, it presents the educated Augustan's view of himself and his world. This view, as Mr. Mack has conclusively shown, was permeated by Renaissance and earlier ideas of order and hierarchy, yet the *Essay* is unmistakably a poem of its period. It is one of many eighteenth-century versions of epic (like, among Pope's own works, the translation of the *Iliad, The Rape of the Lock,* and *The Dunciad*), and, like the two great epics that frame it chronologically, *Paradise Lost* and *The Prelude,* it presents a world view that aroused excitement and conviction among contemporary readers. All three poems show interests typical of their eras: the focus in Milton's is on man's relationship to God, in Pope's on man's relationship to society, and in Wordsworth's on the relationship between man's internal being and physical nature. Yet it is a further irony that while we still retain enough of the Romantic attitude toward life to understand Wordsworth, and enough knowledge, at least, of Christianity to understand Milton, the philosophical basis of Pope's viewpoint has disappeared today. True, some vague notion still persists that the Augustan age was the Age of Reason, and that Pope was its poet, but a more misleading generalization can hardly be found in literary history. The only element of truth in it, as far as the *Essay* is concerned, is that Pope deliberately contrasts its basis to that of *Paradise Lost:* Milton builds on Christian revelation, while Pope builds on reason and experience, fallible indeed as he shows them to be.

Reason manifests itself in the *Essay* as "philosophical optimism," the doctrine that since God is all good he must have created the best of all possible worlds: "WHATEVER IS, IS RIGHT." At first sight, such an idea seems absurd: too much evil exists in the world and in human nature itself to support any such complacent belief. On closer consideration, however, philosophical optimism has its points. Leaving aside the question of physical evil (plagues, earthquakes, etc.) momentarily, it becomes evident that if man has free will, if in Milton's phrase he was created "sufficient to have stood, though free to fall," then the possibility, though not the necessity, of moral evil must exist. God could only have made all men good by denying them free will; in effect, by making them puppets. Furthermore, Pope relies on the traditional belief that out of evil, whether physical or moral, God brings forth good. We can only see part of His grand design, though enough to give us an adequate idea of our place in it. Finally, since God has implanted in man a belief in immortality, and since He does nothing without purpose, we are assured that the wrongs of this world will, if we act our parts properly, be redressed in the next.

Philosophical optimism is the basis of Pope's theodicy (the vindication of God's justice), which is the subject of Epistle I. He embodies it in the traditional concept of the Great Chain of Being: everything in existence is arranged in a hierarchy, which originates in God and ranges through angel, man, beast, plant, to inorganic matter. The idea of the Great Chain of Being commonly involved, as it does here, the principle of plenitude: there are no gaps in the Chain, since God in creating the best of worlds would wish to fill it as full as possible with created entities, each given the attributes appropriate to its place. With every step in the Chain (or every rung on its ladder) occupied, then the basic question for man is where he is located. Here Pope provides the traditional answer that man occupies the place where the rational is combined with the animal. Trouble arises when man's pride leads him to wish to be what he is not: to be discontented because he lacks the "intuitive" reason of the angels (man's being "discursive," or of a trial-and-error nature) and the sensory powers of the animals.

Man must learn to "submit," to realize where he stands in the Chain of Being, and to recognize and fulfill the potentialities that are peculiarly his.

In Epistle II, Pope turns from theodicy to psychology: having shown man's relation to the universe, he now examines man's nature in itself (the first fifty-two lines of the Epistle acting as a transition between the two subjects). The essence of this nature derives from the relation of the rational to the animal, or of reason to the passions, which are modes of self-love. The complex nature of this relationship is indicated by the extraordinary number of analogies Pope invokes to illuminate it: self-love is like the mainspring of a watch, while reason is like its balance; reason is a ship's compass, but self-love is the gale that drives the ship; reason is a weak queen governed by her favorite, the ruling passion; and so forth. Pope never goes so far as Hume does when he declares, "Reason is, and ought only to be, the slave of the passions, and can never pretend to any other office than to serve and obey them." But this Epistle should make plain that Pope did not assert any such naïve idea as that man was fundamentally rational, or that reason could offer the certainty to men in general that revelation does to the Christian.

In his discussion of the reason–passion relationship and elsewhere in the poem, Pope relies on the ancient idea of the *concors discordia rerum:* harmony arises out of the inherent discord or tension among things. He perhaps puts this point most clearly in *Windsor Forest*, where he describes the beauties of the landscape as,

> Not Chaos-like together crushed and bruised,
> But, as the World, harmoniously confused:
> Where Order in Variety we see,
> And where, though all things differ, all agree.

Reconciliation between reason and self-love is achieved through the concept of the "ruling passion," the dominant concern of each individual which gives shape to his character and direction to his actions. Psychology here leads into ethics; if the ruling passion, through the hold it gains on us, is "the Mind's disease" and the foundation of vice, it is also, when guided by reason, the foundation of virtue. Actually, Pope argues, though virtue and vice are not difficult to separate in theory, in practice they are too mingled to be easily distinguished. Yet Heaven so manages it that individual imbalances, in their variety, co-operate to further the purposes of the whole:

> Ev'n mean Self-love becomes, by force divine,
> The scale to measure others' wants by thine.

Epistle III restates the Chain of Being in terms of the inter-dependence of its parts, especially as they are related by mutual need and love; this interdependence fulfills "the gen'ral Good." Each creature has its proper attributes: the animal's instinct is a surer guide than man's reason, yet reason enables man to extend beyond, though not dispense with, his animal nature. Like the animal, he starts from the sexual, "the fierce embrace," but reason expands the instinctive into the habitual, self-love into social love. At this point, Pope summarizes the historical development of society. Originally, men lived in harmony with one another and the animals, whose instinctual activities fur-nished models for their learned ones. Primitive society was patriarchal and mutually productive until its order was vio-lated by tyrants (kings and priests), who molded it to their selfish ends. The need to restrain lawless force, however, prompted the re-establishment of proper government, in which the duties and interests of all men are based on an interde-pendence that mirrors the harmony of the universe described at the Epistle's beginning. Self-love finds not merely its security but its meaning in love of others:

> Man, like the gen'rous vine, supported lives;
> The strength he gains is from th' embrace he gives.

The relationship between Epistle IV and the preceding three has puzzled some readers, since it deals with a mental quality, happiness, and they with man's general nature and state. The relevance of this Epistle becomes apparent if we remember that

Pope here is discussing man, as Aristotle did, in terms of his function, the fulfillment of his potential. Just as it is the shoemaker's function to make shoes, so it is man's function to be happy, to act in accord with what is best in him. Pope starts by rejecting the idea that happiness can exist in extremes of one kind or another, such as Stoicism or Epicureanism, and he maintains that it is natural, social, and independent of fortune. It consists in virtue, and virtue has its own reward: "The soul's calm sunshine and the heartfelt joy." A series of examples follows, showing the defects of those who put their trust in such things as honors, birth, greatness, fame, and natural abilities. Only virtue is self-sufficient, yet it is not selfish: essentially it manifests itself as benevolence, the "charity" of St. Paul. After a nicely turned compliment to Bolingbroke, Pope summarizes the central points of each Epistle in the closing lines, ending with an echo of the poem's opening: to know man's nature, state, and function, it is necessary to know ourselves.

It seems useful to provide this little outline of the *Essay's* content, since, on first reading, its "maze," rather than its plan, commonly stands out. Yet if this paraphrase could be so extended as to do something like justice even to the poem's basic level of meaning, it would hardly suggest why it is such a fine work. Reduced to prose, the *Essay* might arouse mild interest as the rather inconsistent yet serious and suggestive reflections of a man of experience; yet it might equally well be entirely forgotten. In its full poetic form, however, the *Essay* is a brilliant and exciting work, whose complexity begins, at least, to suggest the complexity of existence.

The reasons for the *Essay's* triumph as a poem can only be touched on here: its structural concision, its preciseness of diction and imagery, its modulation of tone, its use of paradox to suggest both contrast and equivalence, its methods of blending abstract and concrete. Some of these points can be illustrated by a brief commentary on Section VII of Epistle I:

Far as Creation's ample range extends,
The scale of sensual, mental pow'rs ascends:

Mark how it mounts, to Man's imperial race,
From the green myriads in the peopled grass: 210
What modes of sight betwixt each wide extreme,
The mole's dim curtain, and the lynx's beam:
Of smell, the headlong lioness between,
And hound sagacious on the tainted green:
Of hearing, from the life that fills the flood,   215
To that which warbles through the vernal wood:
The spider's touch, how exquisitely fine!
Feels at each thread, and lives along the line:
In the nice bee, what sense so subtly true
From pois'nous herbs extracts the healing dew: 220
How Instinct varies in the grov'ling swine,
Compared, half-reas'ning elephant, with thine:
Twixt that, and Reason, what a nice barrier,
For ever sep'rate, yet for ever near!
Remembrance and Reflection how allied;   225
What thin partitions Sense from Thought divide:
And Middle natures, how they long to join,
Yet never pass th' insuperable line!
Without this just gradation, could they be
Subjected, these to those, or all to thee?   230
The pow'rs of all subdued by thee alone,
Is not thy Reason all these pow'rs in one?

This passage is one of many in which Pope embodies the postulates of the Chain of Being. In the preceding lines (I. 193–206), he has argued that if man's senses were made more acute it would only cause him suffering. In the passage quoted, while illustrating the fullness and variety of creation asserted by the principle of plenitude, he wants to demonstrate how the actual range of "sensual, mental pow'rs" on earth culminates and is incorporated in man's reason.

The major technical problem Pope faced here was how to suggest the complexity of this range of powers, couplet by couplet, without retarding the rapid movement which helps to establish the coherence of the passage. In large part, he solves this problem through his handling of structure, syntax, and levels of concreteness of diction and imagery.

The structure is strictly ordered: ll. 207–210 summarize the scene to be depicted; ll. 211–220 describe the range of sensual, and ll. 221–228, of mental powers; and ll. 229–232, which balance the opening four lines, offer the "logical" conclusion to be drawn from this presentation. Syntax powerfully reinforces structure. The imperative tone established by the one main verb, "mark," which governs the whole passage except for its first two and last four lines, is qualified and extended by the exclamatory "how" and "what" constructions of this long sentence: we are not meant to merely observe creation, but to wonder at it.

Structure and syntax might be sufficient in themselves to establish the dominance of the verse paragraph over the units of meaning contained in each couplet, but the relationship of paragraph to couplets is further defined by variation in level of concreteness. The generalized statement of the opening couplet is made only slightly more concrete when specified as the distance between "Man's imperial race" and "the green myriads in the peopled grass." The images are too faint to arrest attention, but they convey a precise meaning. Man is represented as species, not as individual; he is "imperial," of course, because his reason makes him ruler over the animals (with an implicit echo of Genesis). From his point of view, insects are accurately described in periphrasis as "green myriads": living, undifferentiated, uncountable thousands. Yet "peopled" suggests that these extremes of organic being are linked.

In the next five couplets, Pope becomes more concrete as he names particular animals. His descriptions of them appropriately emphasize their powers, not their appearance, and are kept subordinate to their function of illustrating sensory extremes. Yet Pope is not content with mere illustration; in shifting, in the case of the spider, to exemplification of only one extreme, he brings out an underlying idea in the passage—the aliveness and unceasing activity of nature. "Green," used in two senses, has connotations which connect it to "vernal," while the suggestions of "headlong" and "life that fills the flood" help to prepare for the concentration of sensory being, power, and activity in the spider, who "feels at each thread, and lives along the line."[1]

The following lines are a model of skillful transition. The bee's power of discrimination, so subtly accurate as to seem almost rational, emphasizes the unerringness of instinct, which furnishes a pattern for reason (see III. 169 ff.). As the discussion shifts explicitly from the sensual to the mental powers, the swine is contrasted to the "half-reas'ning elephant," but "half-reas'ning" is essentially ironic, since stress in the next lines falls on the closeness of, yet absolute distinction between, the mental powers of man and beast. Appropriately enough, the diction now returns to an abstract level in such words as "Reflection" and "Remembrance." These terms lead easily into the image-less rhetorical questions of the last four lines, whose "logic" and tone of calm, forceful reasonableness "prove" Pope's point.

This passage nicely illustrates Pope's sense of "decorum," the proper adaptation of manner to matter. The metaphysical intensity of Donne, the sensuous particularity of Keats, even the allusiveness of Milton would be out of place here. All is clear apparently; a few words need to be glossed, but even unfamiliar ideas—that fish have little or no sense of hearing, that honey is a dew with medicinal properties—are in effect explained by their context. Yet the clarity of Pope's couplets is a trap; in contrast to the tortuousness of Donne's syntax and imagery which demand concentration if his poetry is to be understood at all, the easy movement of Pope's poetry encourages the idea that the whole has been grasped when only a part, and sometime a small part, has been understood. It is in this sense that Pope is a difficult poet and increasingly rewarding as com-

---

[1] Nor is this all that Pope is doing in these lines. They suggest, for example, how differences in sensory powers are compensated for: the lioness can afford to be "headlong," while the hound needs to be "sagacious." Also, the echo from Genesis is filled out by the mention of fish and birds: God gave Adam dominion over life in all three elements of earth, water, and air.

plexity of meaning and technique unfold themselves. The reader may share George II's reaction as he enters his struggle with the *Essay,* but if he persists he will come to understand the meaning of Dr. Johnson's question: "If Pope be not a poet, where is poetry to be found?"

FRANK BRADY

University Park, Pennsylvania
July 1965

SELECTED BIBLIOGRAPHY

POPE, ALEXANDER. *An Essay on Man*. Edited by MAYNARD MACK. London and New Haven: Methuen and Yale University Press, 1950. (Volume III, Part I of *The Twickenham Edition of the Poems of Alexander Pope*.) The standard text and commentary. It may be supplemented by Mack's introduction to the Roxburghe Club edition of the poem (1962).

ADLER, J. H. "Balance in Pope's Essays," *English Studies*, XLIII (1962), 457–467.

BROWER, REUBEN A. *Alexander Pope: The Poetry of Allusion*. Oxford: Clarendon Press, 1959.

GOLDGAR, BERTRAND A. "Pope's Theory of the Passions: The Background of Epistle II of the *Essay on Man*," *Philological Quarterly*, XLI (1962), 730–743.

HUGHES, R. E. "Pope's *Essay on Man:* The Rhetorical Structure of Epistle I," in *Essential Articles for the Study of Alexander Pope*, edited by MAYNARD MACK. "Archon Books." Hamden, Connecticut: Shoe String, Inc., 1964.

KNIGHT, G. WILSON. *Laureate of Peace*. London: Routledge & Kegan Paul, 1954.

PRICE, MARTIN. *To the Palace of Wisdom*. Garden City, N.Y.: Doubleday, 1964.

TILLOTSON, GEOFFREY. *On the Poetry of Pope*. Oxford: Clarendon Press, 1950.

———. *Pope and Human Nature*. Oxford: Clarendon Press, 1958.

AN ESSAY ON MAN

NOTE ON THE TEXT

AND

ACKNOWLEDGMENTS

Alexander Pope (1688–1744) began to think of writing the *Essay on Man,* or at least of writing some of the Epistles which comprise it, no later than 1729. The first three Epistles were apparently completed by the summer of 1731 and were published individually and anonymously in the winter and spring of 1733. The fourth was completed near the end of 1733 and published in January 1734; in the same year, the four Epistles were first published in a collected edition. Pope continued to revise the poem throughout his life.

The present edition is based on the 1751 large octavo edition of Pope's works edited by William Warburton. Warburton's capitalization has been adhered to, but punctuation has been changed to some extent in the interest of clarity. Spelling forms not recognized by *Webster's Seventh New Collegiate Dictionary* have been modernized, except when modernization seems to involve change of pronunciation. Thus "tost" becomes "tossed," and "ev'ry" becomes "every"; but "nat'ral" is retained. The necessity for indicating ellipsis is ludicrously exemplified by a recent critical primer in which, after printing a line from the *Essay on Criticism* without the proper ellipsis, the author comments on Pope's subtle use of an anapest that he himself created. I have also adhered to Warburton's mixture of what are now British and American spellings. Prose has been normalized throughout.

I am much indebted to critics and previous editors of the *Essay;* where they are quoted directly, their names are appended. I owe a particular and heavy obligation to my teacher, Maynard Mack, and to his definitive Twickenham Edition of the *Essay.* I should also like to thank my friend and former student, Fredric V. Bogel, for his valuable help in preparing this edition for the press and for allowing me to read his fine Dartmouth College honors thesis on the poem.

F.B.

AN ESSAY ON MAN

IN FOUR EPISTLES

TO

HENRY ST. JOHN, LORD BOLINGBROKE

THE DESIGN

Having proposed to write some pieces on human life and manners, such as (to use my Lord Bacon's expression) *come home to men's business and bosoms,* I thought it more satisfactory to begin with considering man in the abstract, his nature and his state; since to prove any moral duty, to enforce any moral precept, or to examine the perfection or imperfection of any creature whatsoever, it is necessary first to know what condition and relation it is placed in, and what is the proper end and purpose of its being.

The science of human nature is, like all other sciences, reduced to a few clear points: there are not many certain truths in this world. It is therefore in the anatomy of the mind as in that of the body; more good will accrue to mankind by attending to the large, open, and perceptible parts than by studying too much such finer nerves and vessels, the conformations and uses of which will forever escape our observation. The disputes are all upon these last, and, I will venture to say, they have less sharpened the wits than the hearts of men against each other, and have diminished the practice, more than advanced the theory, of morality. If I could flatter myself that this *Essay* has any merit, it is in steering betwixt the extremes of doctrines seemingly opposite, in passing over terms utterly unintelligible, and in forming a temperate yet not inconsistent, and a short yet not imperfect system of ethics.

This I might have done in prose, but I chose verse, and even rhyme, for two reasons. The one will appear obvious: that principles, maxims, or precepts so written, both strike the reader more strongly at first, and are more easily retained by him afterwards. The other may seem odd, but is true, I found I could express them more shortly this way than in prose itself; and nothing is more certain than that much of the force as well as grace of arguments or instructions depends on their conciseness. I was unable to treat this part of my subject more in detail, without becoming dry and tedious; or more poetically, without sacrificing perspicuity to ornament, without wandering from the precision, or breaking the chain of reasoning. If any man can unite all these without diminution of any of them, I freely confess he will compass a thing above my capacity.

What is now published is only to be considered as a general map of man, marking out no more than the greater parts, their extent, their limits, and their connection, but leaving the particular to be more fully delineated in the charts which are to follow. Consequently, these Epistles in their progress (if I have health and leisure to make any progress) will be less dry and more susceptible of poetical ornament. I am here only opening the fountains and clearing the passage. To deduce the rivers, to follow them in their course, and to observe their effects, may be a task more agreeable.

EPISTLE I

ARGUMENT

OF THE NATURE AND STATE OF MAN, WITH RESPECT TO THE UNIVERSE

Of man in the abstract. I. That we can judge only with regard to
our own system, being ignorant of the relations of systems and things.
II. That man is not to be deemed imperfect, but a being suited to his
place and rank in the creation, agreeable to the general order of
things, and conformable to ends and relations to him unknown.
III. That it is partly upon his ignorance of future events, and partly
upon the hope of a future state, that all his happiness in the present
depends. IV. The pride of aiming at more knowledge, and pretend-
ing to more perfection, the cause of man's error and misery. The
impiety of putting himself in the place of God, and judging of the
fitness or unfitness, perfection or imperfection, justice or injustice of
his dispensations. V. The absurdity of conceiting himself the final
cause of the creation, or expecting that perfection in the moral world,
which is not in the natural. VI. The unreasonableness of his com-
plaints against Providence, while on the one hand he demands the
perfections of the angels, and on the other the bodily qualifications
of the brutes; though to possess any of the sensitive faculties in a
higher degree would render him miserable. VII. That throughout
the whole visible world, an universal order and gradation in the
sensual and mental faculties is observed, which causes a subordination of creature to creature, and of all creatures to man. The gradations of sense, instinct, thought, reflection, reason; that reason alone
countervails all the other faculties. VIII. How much farther this
order and subordination of living creatures may extend, above and
below us; were any part of which broken, not that part only, but the
whole connected creation must be destroyed. IX. The extravagance,
madness, and pride of such a desire. X. The consequence of all, the
absolute submission due to Providence, both as to our present and
future state.

AWAKE, my ST. JOHN![1] leave all meaner things
To low ambition, and the pride of Kings.
Let us (since Life can little more supply
Than just to look about us and to die)
Expatiate free o'er all this scene of Man;   5
A mighty maze! but not without a plan;
A Wild, where weeds and flow'rs promiscuous shoot,
Or Garden, tempting with forbidden fruit.
Together let us beat this ample field,
Try what the open, what the covert yield;   10
The latent tracts, the giddy heights explore
Of all who blindly creep, or sightless soar;
Eye Nature's walks, shoot Folly as it flies,
And catch the Manners[2] living as they rise;
Laugh where we must, be candid[3] where we can;   15
But vindicate the ways of God to Man.[4]
  I.   Say first, of God above, or Man below,
What can we reason, but from what we know?
Of Man what see we, but his station here,
From which to reason, or to which refer?   20
Through worlds unnumbered though the God be known,
'Tis ours to trace him only in our own.
He,[5] who through vast immensity can pierce,
See worlds on worlds compose one universe,
Observe how system into system runs,   25
What other planets circle other suns,
What varied Being peoples every star,
May tell why Heav'n has made us as we are.

---

[1] Henry St. John, first Viscount Bolingbroke, (1678–1751), English statesman, to whom the poem is addressed.

[2] The feelings, outward appearances, and characteristics of men.

[3] Sympathetic.

[4] Just as l. 8 alludes to Milton's Garden of Eden, so Pope's statement of
the central purpose of the poem recalls Milton's similar assertion in *Paradise Lost*: "And justify the ways of God to men" (I. 26).

[5] God, perhaps an angel, and (sarcastically) man.

But of this frame the bearings, and the ties,
The strong connections, nice[6] dependencies,   30
Gradations just, has thy pervading soul
Looked through? or can a part contain the whole?
   Is the great chain,[7] that draws all to agree,
And drawn supports, upheld by God, or thee?
   II.   Presumptuous Man! the reason wouldst thou find,   35
Why formed so weak, so little, and so blind!
First, if thou canst, the harder[8] reason guess,
Why formed no weaker, blinder, and no less!
Ask of thy mother earth, why oaks are made
Taller or stronger than the weeds they shade?   40
Or ask of yonder argent fields above,
Why Jove's Satellites[9] are less than Jove?[1]
   Of Systems possible, if 'tis confessed
That Wisdom infinite must form the best,
Where all must full or not coherent be,[2]   45
And all that rises, rise in due degree;
Then, in the scale of reas'ning life,[3] 'tis plain
There must be, somewhere, such a rank as Man:
And all the question (wrangle e'er so long)
Is only this, if God has placed him wrong?   50
   Respecting Man, whatever wrong we call,
May, must be right, as relative to all.
In human works, though laboured on with pain,
A thousand movements scarce one purpose gain;
In God's, one single can its end produce;   55
Yet serves to second too some other use.

---

6 Subtle, precise.

7 "The Great Chain of Being"; see Introduction, pp. x–xi.

8 More painful, rather than more difficult.

9 Pronounced *sat-ell'-i-tees.*

1 Literally, the planet Jupiter; figuratively, God in his relation to inferior beings.

2 An allusion to the principle of plenitude; see Introduction, p. x.

3 Beings endowed with reason, i.e., men, angels, and God.

So Man, who here seems principal alone,
Perhaps acts second to some sphere unknown,
Touches some wheel, or verges to some goal;
'Tis but a part we see, and not a whole.   60
　　When the proud steed shall know why Man restrains
His fiery course, or drives him o'er the plains;
When the dull Ox, why now he breaks the clod,
Is now a victim, and now Egypt's God:[4]
Then shall Man's pride and dulness comprehend   65
His actions', passions', being's, use and end;
Why doing, suff'ring, checked, impelled; and why
This hour a slave, the next a deity.
　　Then say not Man's imperfect, Heav'n in fault;
Say rather, Man's as perfect as he ought: 70
His knowledge measured to his state and place,
His time a moment, and a point his space.
If to be perfect in a certain sphere,
What matter, soon or late, or here or there?[5]
The blest today is as completely so,   75
As who began a thousand years ago.
　　III.　Heav'n from all creatures hides the book of Fate,
All but the page prescribed, their present state;
From brutes what men, from men what spirits know:
Or who could suffer Being here below?   80
The lamb thy riot dooms to bleed today,
Had he thy Reason, would he skip and play?
Pleased to the last, he crops the flow'ry food,
And licks the hand just raised to shed his blood.
Oh blindness to the future! kindly giv'n,   85
That each may fill the circle marked by Heav'n:
Who sees with equal eye, as God of all,
A hero perish, or a sparrow fall,[6]
Atoms or systems into ruin hurled,
And now a bubble burst, and now a world.   90

---

4 Apis, the sacred bull of Memphis.
5 Here on earth or there in heaven.
6 See Matthew 10:29–31.

Hope humbly then; with trembling pinions soar;
Wait the great teacher Death, and God adore!
What future bliss, he gives not thee to know,
But gives that Hope to be thy blessing now.
Hope springs eternal in the human breast: 95
Man never Is, but always To be blest:
The soul, uneasy and confined from home,[7]
Rests and expatiates in a life to come.

   Lo! the poor Indian, whose untutored mind
Sees God in clouds, or hears him in the wind; 100
His soul proud Science[8] never taught to stray
Far as the solar walk, or milky way;
Yet simple Nature to his hope has giv'n,
Behind the cloud-topped hill, an humbler heav'n;
Some safer world in depth of woods embraced, 105
Some happier island in the wat'ry waste,
Where slaves once more their native land behold,
No fiends torment, no Christians thirst for gold!
To Be, contents his natural desire,
He asks no Angel's wing, no Seraph's fire;[9] 110
But thinks, admitted to that equal[1] sky,
His faithful dog shall bear him company.

   IV. Go, wiser thou! and in thy scale of sense
Weigh thy Opinion against Providence;
Call Imperfection what thou fancy'st such,
Say, here he gives too little, there too much; 115
Destroy all creatures for thy sport or gust,[2]
Yet cry, If Man's unhappy, God's unjust;
If Man alone ingross not Heav'n's high care,
Alone made perfect here, immortal there: 120
Snatch from his hand the balance and the rod,[3]

---

[7] Heaven.
[8] Latin *scientia*, "knowledge."
[9] "Seraph" is presumably derived from a Hebrew root meaning "to burn."
[1] Equally available to all.
[2] Food (literally, taste).
[3] Respectively, symbols of justice and authority.

Re-judge his justice, be the GOD of GOD!
In Pride, in reas'ning Pride, our error lies;
All quit their sphere, and rush into the skies.
Pride still⁴ is aiming at the blest abodes,   125
Men would be Angels, Angels would be Gods.
Aspiring to be Gods, if Angels fell,
Aspiring to be Angels, Men rebel:
And who but wishes to invert the laws
Of ORDER, sins against th' Eternal Cause.   130
    V.   Ask for what end the heav'nly bodies shine,
Earth for whose use? Pride answers, " 'Tis for mine:
"For me kind Nature wakes her genial⁵ pow'r,
"Suckles each herb, and spreads out every flow'r;
"Annual for me, the grape, the rose renew   135
"The juice nectareous, and the balmy dew;
"For me, the mine a thousand treasures brings;
"For me, health gushes from a thousand springs;
"Seas roll to waft me, suns to light me rise;
"My footstool earth, my canopy the skies."⁶   140
    But errs not Nature from this gracious end,
From burning suns when livid deaths descend,⁷
When earthquakes swallow, or when tempests sweep
Towns to one grave, whole nations to the deep?
"No ('tis replied)⁸ the first Almighty Cause   145
"Acts not by partial, but by gen'ral laws;
"Th' exceptions few; some change since all began,
"And what created perfect?"—Why then Man?
If the great end be human Happiness,
Then Nature deviates; and can Man do less?⁹   150
As much that end a constant course requires

----

⁴ Always.

⁵ Generative.

⁶ See Isaiah 66:1.

⁷ Plagues were thought to be caused by the sun's excessive heat.

⁸ By Pride.

⁹ Just as plagues and earthquakes form part of physical nature, so the possibility of evil forms part of man's moral nature, as Pope points out in ll. 151–164; see Introduction, p. x.

Of show'rs and sunshine, as of Man's desires;
As much eternal springs and cloudless skies,
As Men for ever temp'rate, calm, and wise.
If plagues or earthquakes break not Heav'n's design,   155
Why then a Borgia, or a Catiline?[1]
Who knows but he, whose hand the lightning forms,
Who heaves old Ocean, and who wings the storms,
Pours fierce Ambition in a Caesar's mind,
Or turns young Ammon[2] loose to scourge mankind?   160
From pride, from pride, our very reas'ning springs;
Account for moral as for nat'ral things:
Why charge we Heav'n in those, in these acquit?
In both, to reason right is to submit.

   Better for Us, perhaps, it might appear,   165
Were there all harmony, all virtue here;
That never air or ocean felt the wind;
That never passion discomposed the mind:
But ALL subsists by elemental strife;[3]
And Passions are the elements of Life.   170
The gen'ral ORDER, since the whole began,
Is kept in Nature, and is kept in Man.
   VI.   What would this Man? Now upward will he soar,
And little less than Angel, would be more;
Now looking downwards, just as grieved appears   175
To want the strength of bulls, the fur of bears.
Made for his use all creatures if he call,
Say what their use, had he the pow'rs of all?
Nature to these, without profusion kind,
The proper organs, proper pow'rs assigned;   180
Each seeming want compensated[4] of course,[5]
Here with degrees of swiftness, there of force;

---

1 The Borgias were Italian Renaissance rulers noted for violence, deceit, and depravity. Catiline was a conspirator against the Roman Republic.
2 Alexander the Great.
3 (1) The strife among the four elements; (2) fundamental strife.
4 Pronounced *com-pen'-sa-ted.*
5 "In ordinary or due course"—*Oxford English Dictionary.*

All in exact proportion to the state;
Nothing to add, and nothing to abate.
Each beast, each insect, happy in its own: 185
Is Heav'n unkind to Man, and Man alone?
Shall he alone, whom rational we call,
Be pleased with nothing, if not blessed with all?
   The bliss of Man (could Pride that blessing find)
Is not to act or think beyond mankind;   190
No pow'rs of body or of soul to share,
But what his nature and his state can bear.
Why has not Man a microscopic eye?
For this plain reason, Man is not a Fly.
Say what the use, were finer optics giv'n,   195
T' inspect a mite, not comprehend the heav'n?[6]
Or touch, if tremblingly alive all o'er,
To smart and agonize at every pore?
Or quick effluvia[7] darting through the brain,
Die of a rose in aromatic pain?   200
If nature thundered in his op'ning ears,
And stunned him with the music of the spheres,[8]
How would he wish that Heav'n had left him still
The whisp'ring Zephyr, and the purling rill?
Who finds not Providence all good and wise,   205
Alike in what it gives, and what denies?
   VII.   Far as Creation's ample range extends,
The scale of sensual, mental pow'rs ascends:
Mark how it mounts, to Man's imperial race,
From the green myriads in the peopled grass: 210
What modes of sight betwixt each wide extreme,
The mole's dim curtain, and the lynx's beam:[9]

---

[6] According to tradition, man's vision was given him to contemplate the heavens, not to inspect the infinitesimal. Flies were supposed to have extremely acute sight.

[7] Invisible particles which were thought to carry odors.

[8] The music, audible to angels but not to man, supposedly produced by the motion of the orbs which contained the earth, planets, sun, etc.

[9] According to an early theory of vision, the eye emitted a beam of particles.

Of smell, the headlong lioness between,[1]
And hound sagacious[2] on the tainted[3] green:
Of hearing, from the life that fills the flood,   215
To that which warbles through the vernal wood:
The spider's touch, how exquisitely fine!
Feels at each thread, and lives along the line:
In the nice bee, what sense so subtly true
From pois'nous herbs extracts the healing dew: 220
How Instinct varies in the grov'ling swine,
Compared, half-reas'ning elephant, with thine:
Twixt that, and Reason, what a nice barrier,[4]
For ever sep'rate, yet for ever near!
Remembrance and Reflection[5] how allied;   225
What thin partitions Sense[6] from Thought divide:
And Middle natures, how they long to join,
Yet never pass th' insuperable line![7]
Without this just gradation, could they be
Subjected, these to those, or all to thee?   230
The pow'rs of all subdued by thee alone,
Is not thy Reason all these pow'rs in one?
   VIII.   See, through this air, this ocean, and this earth,
All matter quick,[8] and bursting into birth.
Above, how high progressive life may go!   235
Around, how wide! how deep extend below!
Vast chain of Being, which from God began,
Natures ethereal, human, angel, man,

---

1 According to Pope, lions pursued their prey "by the ear, and not by the nostril."

2 "Acute in perception, esp. by the sense of smell"—*OED*.

3 "Imbued with the scent of an animal (usually a hunted animal)"—*OED*.

4 Here pronounced *bar-reer'*.

5 By "Remembrance," Pope means the power of memory; by "Reflection," the power of introspection. Man alone has "Reflection."

6 The senses.

7 Apparently, "Middle natures" refers to animals intermediate in classification, like frogs and bats, but the sense and syntax of ll. 237–238 are obscure.

8 Pregnant.

Beast, bird, fish, insect! what no eye can see,
No glass can reach! from Infinite to thee,   240
From thee to Nothing!—On superior pow'rs
Were we to press, inferior might on ours:
Or in the full creation leave a void,
Where, one step broken, the great scale's destroyed:
From Nature's chain whatever link you strike,   245
Tenth or ten thousandth, breaks the chain alike.

  And if each system in gradation roll,
Alike essential to th' amazing Whole,
The least confusion but in one, not all
That system only, but the Whole must fall.   250
Let Earth unbalanced from her orbit fly,
Planets and Suns run lawless through the sky,
Let ruling Angels from their spheres be hurled,[9]
Being on Being wrecked, and world on world,
Heav'n's whole foundations to their centre nod,   255
And Nature tremble to the throne of God:
All this dread ORDER break—for whom? for thee?
Vile worm!—oh Madness, Pride, Impiety!
  IX.   What if the foot, ordained the dust to tread,
Or hand, to toil, aspired to be the head?   260
What if the head, the eye, or ear repined
To serve mere engines[1] to the ruling Mind?[2]
Just as absurd for any part to claim
To be another, in this gen'ral frame:
Just as absurd, to mourn the tasks or pains   265
The great directing MIND of ALL ordains.

  All are but parts of one stupendous whole,
Whose body Nature is, and God the soul;
That, changed through all, and yet in all the same,
Great in the earth, as in th' ethereal frame,   270
Warms in the sun, refreshes in the breeze,

---

  [9] According to early cosmology, an "intelligence" or angel moved or
guided each heavenly sphere.
  [1] Mechanical subordinates.
  [2] See I Corinthians 12:12–27.

Glows in the stars, and blossoms in the trees,
Lives through all life, extends through all extent,
Spreads undivided, operates unspent,
Breathes in our soul, informs our mortal part,   275
As full, as perfect, in a hair as heart;
As full, as perfect, in vile Man that mourns,
As the rapt Seraph that adores and burns:
To him no high, no low, no great, no small;
He fills, he bounds, connects, and equals all.[3]   280
   X.   Cease then, nor ORDER Imperfection name:
Our proper bliss depends on what we blame.
Know thy own point: This kind, this due degree
Of blindness, weakness, Heav'n bestows on thee.
Submit—In this, or any other sphere,   285
Secure to be as blest as thou canst bear:
Safe in the hand of one disposing Pow'r,
Or in the natal, or the mortal hour.
All Nature is but Art,[4] unknown to thee;
All Chance, Direction, which thou canst not see;   290
All Discord, Harmony, not understood;
All partial Evil, universal Good:
And, spite of Pride, in erring Reason's spite,
One truth is clear, "WHATEVER IS, IS RIGHT."

---

3 Makes all equal.
4 Alluding to the commonplace that nature is the art of God.

EPISTLE II

Argument

I.   Know then thyself, presume not God to scan;[1]
The proper study of Mankind is Man.
Placed on this isthmus of a middle state,
A Being darkly wise, and rudely great:
With too much knowledge for the Sceptic side,[2]   5
With too much weakness for the Stoic's pride,
He hangs between; in doubt to act, or rest,
In doubt to deem himself a God, or Beast;[3]

---

1 Criticize.

2 With too much knowledge to be a Skeptic. Skepticism was a Greek philosophical theory which denied that real knowledge was attainable.

3 In ll. 7–8, Pope sets up as extremes the active pleasure-seeking popularly attributed to Epicureanism and the proud withdrawal from action considered characteristic of Stoicism.

In doubt his Mind or Body to prefer,
Born but to die, and reas'ning but to err;   10
Alike in ignorance, his reason such,
Whether he thinks too little, or too much:
Chaos of Thought and Passion, all confused;
Still by himself abused, or disabused;
Created half to rise, and half to fall;   15
Great lord of all things, yet a prey to all;
Sole judge of Truth, in endless Error hurled:[4]
The glory, jest, and riddle of the world!
    Go, wondrous creature! mount where Science[5] guides,
Go, measure earth, weigh air, and state the tides;   20
Instruct the planets in what orbs to run,
Correct old Time, and regulate the Sun;[6]
Go, soar with Plato to th' empyreal sphere,
To the first good, first perfect, and first fair;[7]
Or tread the mazy round his follow'rs trod,   25
And quitting sense call imitating God;[8]
As Eastern priests in giddy circles run,
And turn their heads to imitate the Sun.
Go, teach Eternal Wisdom how to rule—
Then drop into thyself, and be a fool!   30
    Superior beings, when of late they saw
A mortal Man unfold all Nature's law,
Admired such wisdom in an earthly shape,

---

[4] "To *hurl* signifies not simply to cast, but to cast backward and forward, and is taken from the rural game called hurling"—Warburton.

[5] Not merely science in the modern sense, but all branches of knowledge and investigation. The ironic meaning of l. 20 is established by reference to Isaiah 40:12.

[6] Apparently a reference to certain of Newton's astronomical theories.

[7] Pope locates Plato's archetypal Ideas of Goodness, Truth, and Beauty in the empyrean—the highest sphere in ancient cosmology and the heavenly paradise.

[8] An allusion to the Neoplatonic desire to transcend the flesh. "Sense" means both common sense and the sensory.

And showed a NEWTON as we show an Ape.[9]
  Could he, whose rules the rapid Comet bind,   35
Describe or fix one movement of his Mind?
Who saw its fires here rise, and there descend,[1]
Explain his own beginning, or his end?
Alas what wonder! Man's superior part
Unchecked may rise, and climb from art to art: 40
But when his own great work is but begun,
What Reason weaves, by Passion is undone.[2]
  Trace Science then, with Modesty thy guide;
First strip off all her equipage of Pride,
Deduct what is but Vanity, or Dress,   45
Or Learning's Luxury, or Idleness;[3]
Or tricks to show the stretch of human brain,
Mere curious pleasure, or ingenious pain:
Expunge the whole, or lop th' excrescent parts
Of all, our Vices have created Arts: 50
Then see how little the remaining sum,
Which served the past, and must the times to come!
  II.   Two Principles in human nature reign;
Self-love, to urge, and Reason, to restrain;
Nor this a good, nor that a bad we call,   55
Each works its end, to move or govern all:
And to their proper operation still,
Ascribe all Good; to their improper, Ill.
  Self-love, the spring of motion, acts[4] the soul;
Reason's comparing balance rules the whole.   60

---

9 The double attitude taken toward Newton in these lines may be contrasted to that of Pope's epitaph for him: "Nature and Nature's Laws lay hid in Night. / God said, Let Newton be! and All was Light."

1 "That is, saw, as it were, both the terminating points of such vast lines as the greater axes of orbits, so immeasurably extended through pure space" —Wakefield.

2 "Sometimes man does use his reason, but to no more lasting purpose than the weaving of Penelope"—Tillotson.

3 "I.e. what is done by learning after a fashion intended to make a show or to save trouble"—Ward.

4 Sets into action.

Man, but for that, no action could attend,[5]
And, but for this, were active to no end:
Fixed like a plant on his peculiar spot,
To draw nutrition, propagate, and rot;
Or, meteor-like, flame lawless through the void,   65
Destroying others, by himself destroyed.
  Most strength the moving principle requires;
Active its task, it prompts, impels, inspires.
Sedate and quiet the comparing lies,
Formed but to check, delib'rate, and advise.   70
Self-love still stronger, as its objects nigh;
Reason's at distance, and in prospect lie:
That sees immediate good by present sense;
Reason, the future and the consequence.
Thicker than arguments, temptations throng,   75
At best more watchful this, but that more strong.
The action of the stronger to suspend
Reason still use, to Reason still attend:
Attention, habit and experience gains;[6]
Each strengthens Reason, and Self-love restrains.   80
  Let subtle schoolmen[7] teach these friends to fight,
More studious to divide than to unite.
And Grace and Virtue, Sense and Reason split,
With all the rash dexterity of Wit:
Wits, just like Fools, at war about a name,   85
Have full as oft no meaning, or the same.
Self-love and Reason to one end aspire,
Pain their aversion, Pleasure their desire;
But greedy That, its object would devour,
This taste the honey, and not wound the flow'r: 90
Pleasure, or wrong or rightly understood,
Our greatest evil, or our greatest good.

---

  [5] Apply himself to.

  [6] Attention (the power of concentration) becomes reinforced by habit and experience.

  [7] Strictly speaking, Scholastic philosophers of the Middle Ages, but applied here to all theological and ethical hairsplitters.

III. Modes of Self-love the Passions we may call;
'Tis real good, or seeming, moves them all;
But since not every good we can divide,   95
And Reason bids us for our own provide;
Passions, though selfish, if their means be fair,
List[8] under Reason, and deserve her care;
Those, that imparted, court a nobler aim,
Exalt their kind, and take some Virtue's name.   100
    In lazy Apathy[9] let Stoics boast
Their Virtue fixed; 'tis fixed as in a frost,
Contracted all, retiring to the breast;
But strength of mind is Exercise, not Rest:
The rising tempest puts in act the soul,   105
Parts it may ravage, but preserves the whole.
On life's vast ocean diversely we sail,
Reason the card,[1] but Passion is the gale;
Nor God alone in the still calm we find,
He mounts the storm, and walks upon the wind.[2]   110
    Passions, like Elements, though born to fight,
Yet, mixed and softened, in his work unite:
These 'tis enough to temper and employ;
But what composes Man, can Man destroy?
Suffice that Reason keep to Nature's road,   115
Subject, compound them, follow her and God.
Love, Hope, and Joy, fair pleasure's smiling train,
Hate, Fear, and Grief, the family of pain,
These mixed with art and to due bounds confined,
Make and maintain the balance of the mind: 120
The lights and shades, whose well-accorded strife
Gives all the strength and colour of our life.
    Pleasures are ever in our hands or eyes,
And when in act they cease, in prospect rise:

---

8 Enlist.
9 From Greek *apatheia*, "without feeling."
1 The compass. According to Mack, "the meaning should probably include the mariner's chart or map."
2 A reminiscence of various Biblical passages, such as Psalms 104:3.

Present to grasp, and future still to find,   125
The whole employ of body and of mind.
All spread their charms, but charm not all alike;
On diff'rent senses diff'rent objects strike;
Hence diff'rent Passions more or less inflame,
As strong or weak, the organs of the frame;   130
And hence one MASTER PASSION in the breast,
Like Aaron's serpent, swallows up the rest.[3]
   As Man, perhaps, the moment of his breath,
Receives the lurking principle of death;
The young disease, that must subdue at length,   135
Grows with his growth, and strengthens with his strength:
So, cast and mingled with his very frame,
The Mind's disease, its RULING PASSION came;
Each vital humour[4] which should feed the whole,
Soon flows to this, in body and in soul: 140
Whatever warms the heart, or fills the head,
As the mind opens, and its functions spread,
Imagination plies her dang'rous art,
And pours it all upon the peccant part.[5]
   Nature its[6] mother, Habit is its nurse;   145
Wit, Spirit, Faculties,[7] but make it worse;
Reason itself but gives it edge and pow'r;
As Heav'n's blest beam turns vinegar more sour.
We, wretched subjects though to lawful sway,
In this weak queen some fav'rite still obey.   150
Ah! if she lend not arms, as well as rules,
What can she more than tell us we are fools?
Teach us to mourn our Nature, not to mend,

---

   [3] Aaron's rod, turned into a serpent, swallowed the similarly metamorphosed rods of the Egyptian magicians (Exodus 7:10–12).

   [4] Apparently "the several sorts of 'spirits'—natural, vital, animal—that in the old physiology were credited with nourishing the powers of body and soul"—Mack.

   [5] The morally disruptive imagination strengthens the diseased ruling passion.

   [6] The ruling passion's.

   [7] Powers of the mind or, perhaps more generally, aptitudes, abilities.

A sharp accuser, but a helpless friend!
Or from a judge turn pleader, to persuade   155
The choice we make, or justify it made;
Proud of an easy conquest all along,
She but removes weak passions for the strong:
So, when small humours gather to a gout,
The doctor fancies he has driv'n them out.[8]   160
   Yes, Nature's road must ever be preferred;[9]
Reason is here no guide, but still a guard:
'Tis hers to rectify, not overthrow,
And treat this passion more as friend than foe:
A mightier Pow'r the strong direction sends,   165
And sev'ral[1] Men impels to sev'ral ends.
Like varying winds, by other passions tossed,
This drives them constant to a certain coast.
Let pow'r or knowledge, gold or glory, please,
Or (oft more strong than all), the love of ease;   170
Through life 'tis followed, ev'n at life's expense;
The merchant's toil, the sage's indolence,
The monk's humility, the hero's pride,
All, all alike, find Reason on their side.
   Th' Eternal Art educing good from ill,   175
Grafts on this Passion our best principle:
'Tis thus the Mercury of Man[2] is fixed,
Strong grows the Virtue with his nature mixed;
The dross cements what else were too refined,
And in one interest body acts with mind.   180
   As fruits ungrateful[3] to the planter's care
On savage stocks inserted learn to bear,

---

8 Gout was thought both to result from a collection of "humours" and to drive out all other diseases.

9 Here given its older pronunciation to rhyme with "guard." Cf. the rhyme in II. 9–10.

1 Different.

2 Man's unstable character. The metaphor is drawn from contemporary chemistry.

3 "Not responding to cultivation"—*OED*.

The surest Virtues thus from Passions shoot,
Wild Nature's vigor working at the root.
What crops of wit and honesty appear   185
From spleen, from obstinacy, hate, or fear!
See anger, zeal and fortitude supply;
Ev'n av'rice, prudence; sloth, philosophy;
Lust, through some certain strainers[4] well refined,
Is gentle love, and charms all womankind;   190
Envy, to which th' ignoble mind's a slave,
Is emulation in the learned or brave;
Nor Virtue, male or female, can we name,
But what will grow on Pride, or grow on Shame.

   Thus Nature gives us (let it check our pride)   195
The virtue nearest to our vice allied:
Reason the bias[5] turns to good from ill,
And Nero reigns a Titus,[6] if he will.
The fiery soul abhorred in Catiline,
In Decius charms, in Curtius is divine:[7]   200
The same ambition can destroy or save,
And makes a patriot[8] as it makes a knave.
   IV.   This light and darkness in our chaos joined,[9]
What shall divide? The God within the mind.

   Extremes in Nature equal ends produce,[1]   205
In Man they join to some mysterious use;
Though each by turns the other's bound invade,

---

4 As Dixon points out, the image seems derived from horticulture, strainers being the natural sieves or filters by which plants obtain water.

5 The irregularity in shape that causes a bowl to roll in one direction or another in the game of lawn bowls.

6 Virtuous Roman emperor (r. 79–81).

7 Two Roman heroes who sacrificed themselves for the good of their country.

8 As well as having its modern meaning, "patriot" meant a member of the Opposition in Parliament, which Pope supported.

9 *Oi*, as in "joined," seems to have been pronounced *i* in Pope's time.

1 Produce comparable or equivalent ends. A reference to the " 'reconciled extremes' of drought and rain [etc.] . . . on which, in the traditional view, the well-being of the world is founded"—Mack.

As, in some well-wrought picture, light and shade,
And oft so mix, the diff'rence is too nice
Where ends the Virtue, or begins the Vice.   210
    Fools! who from hence into the notion fall,
That Vice or Virtue there is none at all.
If white and black blend, soften, and unite
A thousand ways, is there no black or white?
Ask your own heart, and nothing is so plain;   215
'Tis to mistake them, costs the time and pain.
    V.   Vice is a monster of so frightful mien,
As, to be hated, needs but to be seen;
Yet seen too oft, familiar with her face,
We first endure, then pity, then embrace.   220
But where th' Extreme of Vice, was ne'er agreed:
Ask where's the North? at York, 'tis on the Tweed;[2]
In Scotland, at the Orcades;[3] and there,
At Greenland, Zembla, or the Lord knows where:
No creature owns it in the first degree,   225
But thinks his neighbour farther gone than he.
Ev'n those who dwell beneath its very zone,
Or never feel the rage, or never own;
What happier natures shrink at with affright,
The hard inhabitant contends is right.   230
    VI.   Virtuous and vicious every Man must be,
Few in th' extreme, but all in the degree;
The rogue and fool by fits is fair and wise;
And ev'n the best, by fits, what they despise.
'Tis but by parts we follow good or ill,   235
For, Vice or Virtue, Self directs it still;
Each individual seeks a sev'ral goal;
But HEAV'N's great view is One, and that the Whole:
That counterworks each folly and caprice;
That disappoints th' effect of every vice;   240
That happy frailties to all ranks applied,

---

[2] The river dividing England from Scotland.
[3] The Orkney Islands, north of the Scottish mainland.

Shame to the virgin, to the matron pride,
Fear to the statesman, rashness to the chief,
To kings presumption, and to crowds belief:
That Virtue's ends from Vanity can raise,   245
Which seeks no int'rest,[4] no reward but praise;
And build on wants, and on defects of mind,
The joy, the peace, the glory of Mankind.
  Heav'n forming each on other to depend,
A master, or a servant, or a friend,   250
Bids each on other for assistance call,
Till one Man's weakness grows the strength of all.
Wants, frailties, passions, closer still ally
The common int'rest, or endear the tie:
To these we owe true friendship, love sincere,   255
Each home-felt joy that life inherits here:
Yet from the same we learn, in its decline,
Those joys, those loves, those int'rests to resign:
Taught half by Reason, half by mere decay,
To welcome death, and calmly pass away.   260
  Whate'er the Passion, knowledge, fame, or pelf,
Not one will change his neighbour with himself.
The learned is happy nature to explore,
The fool is happy that he knows no more;
The rich is happy in the plenty giv'n,   265
The poor contents him with the care of Heav'n.[5]
See the blind beggar dance, the cripple sing,
The sot a hero, lunatic a king;
The starving chemist in his golden views[6]
Supremely blest, the poet in his Muse.   270
  See some strange comfort every state attend,
And Pride bestowed on all, a common friend;
See some fit Passion every age supply,
Hope travels through, nor quits us when we die.
  Behold the child, by Nature's kindly law,   275

---

4 Which has no self-interested view.
5 A reference to Matthew 5:3 and other Biblical passages.
6 The alchemist, who hopes to turn base metals into gold.

Pleased with a rattle, tickled with a straw;
Some livelier plaything gives his youth delight,
A little louder, but as empty quite;
Scarfs, garters,[7] gold, amuse[8] his riper stage;
And beads and prayer books are the toys of age: 280
Pleased with this bauble still, as that before;
Till tired he sleeps, and Life's poor play is o'er!
  Meanwhile Opinion gilds with varying rays
Those painted clouds that beautify our days;
Each want of happiness by Hope supplied,   285
And each vacuity of sense by Pride:
These build as fast as knowledge can destroy;
In Folly's cup still laughs the bubble,[9] joy;
One prospect lost, another still we gain;
And not a vanity is giv'n in vain;   290
Ev'n mean Self-love becomes, by force divine,
The scale to measure others' wants by thine.
See! and confess, one comfort still must rise,
'Tis this, Though Man's a fool, yet GOD IS WISE.

---

7 "Scarfs" refer to those worn by noblemen's chaplains; "garters," to the Order of the Garter and other decorations.

8 Deceive by distracting the attention of.

9 In addition to its literal meaning, "bubble" means "deception."

EPISTLE III

ARGUMENT

OF THE NATURE AND STATE OF MAN, WITH RESPECT TO SOCIETY

I. The whole universe one system of society. Nothing made wholly for itself, nor yet wholly for another. The happiness of animals mutual. II. Reason or Instinct operate alike to the good of each individual. Reason or Instinct operate also to society, in all animals. III. How far society carried by instinct. How much farther by reason. IV. Of that which is called the state of nature. Reason instructed by instinct in the invention of arts, and in the forms of society. V. Origin of political societies. Origin of monarchy. Patriarchal government. VI. Origin of true religion and government, from the same principle, of love. Origin of superstition and tyranny, from the same principle, of fear. The influence of self-love operating to the social and public good. Restoration of true religion and government on their first principle. Mixed government. Various forms of each and the true end of all.

HERE then we rest: "The Universal Cause
"Acts to one end,[1] but acts by various laws."
In all the madness of superfluous health,
The trim of pride, the impudence of wealth,
Let this great truth be present night and day;   5
But most be present, if we preach or pray.
   I. Look round our World; behold the chain of Love
Combining all below and all above.
See plastic[2] Nature working to this end,
The single atoms each to other tend,   10

---

  1 The good of all.

  2 "In a quasi-philosophical sense, as an attribute of an alleged . . . force in nature; formative, procreative"—*OED*.

Attract, attracted to, the next in place
Formed and impelled its neighbour to embrace.
See Matter next, with various life endued,
Press to our centre still, the gen'ral Good.
See dying vegetables life sustain,   15
See life dissolving vegetate again:
All forms that perish other forms supply,
(By turns we catch the vital breath, and die)
Like bubbles on the sea of Matter born,
They rise, they break, and to that sea return.   20
Nothing is foreign: Parts relate to whole;
One all-extending, all-preserving Soul
Connects each being, greatest with the least;
Made Beast in aid of Man, and Man of Beast;
All served, all serving! nothing stands alone;   25
The chain holds on, and where it ends, unknown.
  Has God, thou fool! worked solely for thy good,
Thy joy, thy pastime, thy attire, thy food?
Who for thy table feeds the wanton fawn,
For him as kindly spread the flow'ry lawn.   30
Is it for thee the lark ascends and sings?
Joy tunes his voice, joy elevates his wings.
Is it for thee the linnet pours his throat?
Loves of his own and raptures swell the note.
The bounding steed you pompously bestride,   35
Shares with his lord the pleasure and the pride.
Is thine alone the seed that strews the plain?
The birds of heav'n shall vindicate[3] their grain.
Thine the full harvest of the golden year?
Part pays, and justly, the deserving steer.   40
The hog, that plows not nor obeys thy call,
Lives on the labours of this lord of all.
  Know, Nature's children all divide her care;
The fur that warms a monarch, warmed a bear.
While Man exclaims, "See all things for my use!"   45
"See man for mine!" replies a pampered goose:

---

[3] Lay claim to, as their rightful property.

And just as short of reason He must fall,
Who thinks all made for one, not one for all.
  Grant that the pow'rful still the weak control,
Be Man the Wit[4] and Tyrant of the whole: 50
Nature that Tyrant checks; he only knows,
And helps, another creature's wants and woes.
Say, will the falcon, stooping from above,
Smit with her varying plumage, spare the dove?
Admires the jay the insect's gilded wings?   55
Or hears the hawk when Philomela[5] sings?
Man cares for all: to birds he gives his woods,
To beasts his pastures, and to fish his floods;
For some his Int'rest prompts him to provide,
For more his pleasure, yet for more his pride: 60
All feed on one vain Patron, and enjoy
Th' extensive blessing of his luxury.[6]
That very life his learned[7] hunger craves,
He saves from famine, from the savage[8] saves;
Nay, feasts the animal he dooms his feast,   65
And, till he ends the being, makes it blest;
Which sees no more the stroke, or feels the pain,
Than favoured Man by touch ethereal slain.[9]
The creature had his feast of life before;
Thou too must perish, when thy feast is o'er!   70
  To each unthinking being, Heav'n a friend,
Gives not the useless knowledge of its end:
To Man imparts it; but with such a view
As, while he dreads it, makes him hope it too:
The hour concealed, and so remote the fear,   75

---

4 The one earthly creature endowed with reason.
5 The nightingale.
6 Extravagance.
7 Artificial, not arising from nature.
8 Beast.
9 "Several of the ancients, and many of the Orientals since, esteemed those who were struck by lightning as sacred persons and the particular favourites of Heaven"—Pope.

Death still draws nearer, never seeming near.
Great standing miracle! that Heav'n assigned
Its only thinking thing this turn of mind.
   II.   Whether with Reason, or with Instinct blest,
Know, all enjoy that pow'r which suits them best;   80
To bliss alike by that direction tend,
And find the means proportioned to their end.
Say, where full Instinct is th' unerring guide,
What Pope or Council[1] can they need beside?
Reason, however able, cool at best,   85
Cares not for service, or but serves when pressed,[2]
Stays till we call, and then not often near;
But honest Instinct comes a volunteer,
Sure never to o'ershoot, but just to hit,
While still too wide or short is human Wit;   90
Sure by quick Nature happiness to gain,
Which heavier Reason labours at in vain.
This too serves always, Reason never long;
One must go right, the other may go wrong.
See then the acting and comparing pow'rs   95
One in their nature, which are two in ours;
And Reason raise o'er Instinct as you can,
In this 'tis God directs, in that 'tis Man.
   Who taught the nations of the field and wood[3]
To shun their poison, and to choose their food?   100
Prescient, the tides or tempests to withstand,
Build on the wave, or arch beneath the sand?[4]
Who made the spider parallels design,
Sure as Demoivre,[5] without rule or line?
Who bid the stork, Columbus-like, explore   105

---

[1] "The Roman Catholic council, which claims to be infallible"—Elwin-Courthope.

[2] Impressed, forced into naval service.

[3] Corrected to "flood" in an early erratum slip, but not changed in later editions.

[4] As Mack points out, both modes of nesting attributed to the halcyon, or kingfisher.

[5] Abraham Demoivre (1667–1754), a French mathematician.

Heav'ns not his own, and worlds unknown before?
Who calls the council, states the certain day,
Who forms the phalanx, and who points the way?
   III.   God, in the nature of each being, founds
Its proper bliss, and sets its proper bounds: 110
But as he framed a Whole, the Whole to bless,
On mutual Wants built mutual Happiness:
So from the first, eternal ORDER ran,
And creature linked to creature, man to man.
Whate'er of life all-quick'ning ether keeps,[6]   115
Or breathes through air, or shoots beneath the deeps,
Or pours profuse on earth, one nature feeds
The vital flame,[7] and swells the genial[8] seeds.
Not Man alone, but all that roam the wood,
Or wing the sky, or roll along the flood,   120
Each loves itself, but not itself alone,
Each sex desires alike, till two are one.
Nor ends the pleasure with the fierce embrace;
They love themselves, a third time, in their race.
Thus beast and bird their common charge attend,   125
The mothers nurse it, and the sires defend;
The young dismissed to wander earth or air,
There stops the Instinct, and there ends the care;
The link dissolves, each seeks a fresh embrace,
Another love succeeds, another race.   130
A longer care Man's helpless kind demands;
That longer care contracts more lasting bands:
Reflection, Reason, still the ties improve,
At once extend the int'rest, and the love;
With choice we fix, with sympathy we burn;   135
Each Virtue in each Passion takes its turn;
And still new needs, new helps, new habits rise,

---

6 Keeps in itself. According to Pope, "the ancient philosophers supposed
the ether to be igneous, and by its kind influence upon the air to be the
cause of all vegetation"—*Iliad* I. 514 n.

7 A substance constituting life, thought literally to exist within animals.

8 Generative.

That graft benevolence on charities.[9]
Still as one brood, and as another rose,
These nat'ral love maintained, habitual those: 140
The last, scarce ripened into perfect Man,
Saw helpless him from whom their life began:
Mem'ry and forecast just returns engage,
That pointed back to youth, this on to age;
While pleasure, gratitude, and hope, combined,   145
Still spread the int'rest, and preserved the kind.
   IV.   Nor think, in NATURE's STATE they blindly trod;
The state of Nature was the reign of God:[1]
Self-love and Social at her birth began,
Union the bond of all things, and of Man.   150
Pride then was not; nor Arts, that Pride to aid;
Man walked with beast, joint tenant of the shade;
The same his table, and the same his bed;
No murder clothed him, and no murder fed.
In the same temple, the resounding wood,   155
All vocal beings hymned their equal God:
The shrine with gore unstained, with gold undressed,
Unbribed, unbloody, stood the blameless priest:
Heav'n's attribute was Universal Care,
And Man's prerogative to rule, but spare.   160
Ah! how unlike the man of times to come!
Of half that live the butcher and the tomb;[2]
Who, foe to Nature, hears the gen'ral groan,
Murders their species, and betrays his own.
But just disease to luxury succeeds,   165
And every death its own avenger breeds;
The Fury-passions from that blood began,

---

9 That graft an habitual attitude of fellow-feeling ("benevolence") on instinctive affections ("charities"). See "nat'ral love" and "habitual" (III. 140).

1 Pope takes the "soft" view of primitive times, seeing them as the Golden Age, rather than the "hard" view of Hobbes and others that life for primitive man was "nasty, brutish, and short."

2 Because he kills and eats animals.

And turned on Man a fiercer savage, Man.
   See him from Nature rising slow to Art!
To copy Instinct then was Reason's part;   170
Thus then to Man the voice of Nature spake—
"Go, from the Creatures thy instructions take:
"Learn from the birds what food the thickets yield;
"Learn from the beasts the physic of the field;[3]
"Thy arts of building from the bee receive;   175
"Learn of the mole to plow, the worm to weave;
"Learn of the little Nautilus to sail,
"Spread the thin oar, and catch the driving gale.[4]
"Here too all forms of social union find,
"And hence let Reason, late, instruct Mankind: 180
"Here subterranean works and cities see;
"There towns aerial on the waving tree.
"Learn each small People's genius, policies,[5]
"The Ant's republic, and the realm of Bees;
"How those in common all their wealth bestow,   185
"And Anarchy without confusion know;
"And these for ever, though a Monarch reign,
"Their sep'rate cells and properties maintain.
"Mark what unvaried laws preserve each state,
"Laws wise as Nature, and as fixed as Fate.   190
"In vain thy Reason finer webs shall draw,
"Entangle Justice in her net of Law,
"And right, too rigid, harden into wrong;
"Still for the strong too weak, the weak too strong.
"Yet go! and thus o'er all the creatures sway,   195
"Thus let the wiser make the rest obey;
"And, for those Arts mere[6] Instinct could afford,

---

3 The medicinal value of herbs, etc.

4 The nautiluses "swim on the surface of the sea, on the backs of their shells, which exactly resemble the hulk of a ship; they raise two feet like masts and extend a membrane between, which serves as a sail; the other two feet they employ as oars at the side"—Pope.

5 Wisdom in managing affairs, especially governmental ones.

6 "Mere" seems to have both its early meaning, "pure," and its modern one, the latter ironically reflecting man's attitude toward instinct.

"Be crowned as Monarchs, or as Gods adored."
   V.   Great Nature spoke; observant Men obeyed;
Cities were built, Societies were made: 200
Here rose one little state; another near
Grew by like means, and joined, through love or fear.
Did here the trees with ruddier burdens bend,
And there the streams in purer rills descend?
What War could ravish, Commerce could bestow,[7]   205
And he returned a friend, who came a foe.
Converse and Love mankind might strongly draw,
When Love was Liberty,[8] and Nature Law.
Thus States were formed; the name of King unknown,
Till common int'rest placed the sway in one.   210
'Twas VIRTUE ONLY (or in arts or arms,
Diffusing blessings, or averting harms)
The same which in a Sire the Sons obeyed,
A Prince the Father of a People made.
   VI.   Till then, by Nature crowned, each Patriarch sate, 215
King, priest, and parent of his growing state;
On him, their second Providence, they hung,
Their law his eye, their oracle his tongue.
He from the wond'ring[9] furrow called the food,
Taught to command the fire, control the flood,   220
Draw forth the monsters of th' abyss profound,
Or fetch th' aerial eagle to the ground.
Till drooping, sick'ning, dying, they began
Whom they revered as God to mourn as Man:
Then, looking up from sire to sire, explored[1]   225
One great first father, and that first adored.
Or plain tradition that this All begun,

---

   [7] Impart willingly.
   [8] "When men had no need to guard their native liberty from their governors by civil factions: the love which each master of a family had for those under his care being their best security"—Warburton.
   [9] Possibly a transferred epithet, describing the people rather than the furrow.
   [1] Found by searching.

Conveyed unbroken faith from sire to son;
The worker from the work distinct was known,
And simple Reason never sought but one: 230
Ere Wit oblique had broke that steady light,[2]
Man, like his Maker, saw that all was right;[3]
To Virtue, in the paths of Pleasure, trod,
And owned a Father when he owned a God.
Love all the faith, and all th' allegiance then;   235
For Nature knew no right divine[4] in Men,
No ill could fear in God: and understood
A sov'reign being but a sov'reign good.
True faith, true policy, united ran,
That was but love of God, and this of Man.   240
    Who first taught souls enslaved, and realms undone,
Th' enormous[5] faith of many made for one;[6]
That proud exception to all Nature's laws,
T' invert the world, and counterwork its Cause?
Force first made Conquest, and that conquest, Law;   245
Till Superstition taught the tyrant awe,
Then shared the Tyranny, then lent it aid,
And Gods of Conqu'rors, Slaves of Subjects made:
She, midst the lightning's blaze, and thunder's sound,
When rocked the mountains, and when groaned the ground,
She taught the weak to bend, the proud to pray,   251
To Pow'r unseen, and mightier far than they:
She, from the rending earth and bursting skies,
Saw Gods descend, and fiends infernal rise:
Here fixed the dreadful, there the blest abodes;   255
Fear made her Devils, and weak Hope her Gods;

---

2 "A beautiful allusion to the effects of the prismatic glass on the rays of light"—Warburton.

3 See Genesis 1:31.

4 An allusion to the theory that kings ruled by "divine right."

5 Deviating from the norm, monstrous; hence, wicked.

6 "In this Aristotle placeth the difference between a king and a tyrant, that the first supposeth himself made for the people; the other, that the people are made for him"—Warburton.

Gods partial, changeful, passionate, unjust,
Whose attributes were Rage, Revenge, or Lust;
Such as the souls of cowards might conceive,
And, formed like tyrants, tyrants would believe.   260
Zeal[7] then, not charity, became the guide,
And hell was built on spite, and heav'n on pride.
Then sacred seemed th' ethereal vault no more;
Altars grew marble then, and reeked with gore:
Then first the Flamen tasted living food;   265
Next his grim idol smeared with human blood;
With Heav'n's own thunders shook the world below,
And played the God an engine on his foe.
    So drives Self-love, through just and through unjust,
To one Man's pow'r, ambition, lucre, lust: 270
The same Self-love, in all, becomes the cause
Of what restrains him, Government and Laws.
For, what one likes if others like as well,
What serves one will, when many wills rebel?[8]
How shall he keep, what, sleeping or awake,   275
A weaker may surprise, a stronger take?
His safety must his liberty restrain:
All join to guard what each desires to gain.
Forced into virtue thus by Self-defence,
Ev'n Kings learned justice and benevolence: 280
Self-love forsook the path it first pursued,
And found the private in the public good.
    'Twas then, the studious head or gen'rous mind,
Follow'r of God or friend of humankind,
Poet[9] or Patriot, rose but to restore   285
The Faith and Moral,[1] Nature gave before;
Relumed her ancient light, not kindled new;
If not God's image, yet his shadow drew:
Taught Pow'r's due use to People and to Kings,

---

7 Fanaticism.
8 How powerful can one will be, when many wills rebel against it?
9 Seen in his traditional role as legislator of mankind.
1 Morality.

Taught nor to slack, nor strain its tender strings,   290
The less, or greater, set so justly true,
That touching one must strike[2] the other too;
Till jarring int'rests of themselves create
Th' according music of a well-mixed State.[3]
Such is the World's great harmony, that springs   295
From Order, Union, full Consent of things!
Where small and great, where weak and mighty, made
To serve, not suffer, strengthen, not invade,
More pow'rful each as needful to the rest,
And, in proportion as it blesses, blest,   300
Draw to one point, and to one centre bring
Beast, Man, or Angel, Servant, Lord, or King.
    For Forms of Government let fools contest;
Whate'er is best administered is best:[4]
For Modes of Faith let graceless zealots fight;   305
His can't be wrong whose life is in the right:
In Faith and Hope the world will disagree,
But all Mankind's concern is Charity:[5]
All must be false that thwart this One great End,
And all of God, that bless Mankind or mend.   310
    Man, like the gen'rous vine, supported lives;
The strength he gains is from th' embrace he gives.[6]
On their own Axis as the Planets run,
Yet make at once their circle round the Sun:

---

2 Cause to reverberate.

3 "Mixed government" was a popular phrase to describe the system of checks and balances among the King, Lords, and Commons in eighteenth-century Britain.

4 Pope later defended these lines by writing that "the author . . . was far from meaning that no one form of government is, in itself, better than another . . . but that no form of government, however excellent or preferable in itself, can be sufficient to make a people happy, unless it be administered with integrity."

5 See I Corinthians 13:13.

6 The marriage and reciprocal support of elm and vine has been a rhetorical commonplace since Catullus. "Gen'rous" here means something like "giving oneself freely or magnanimously."

So two consistent motions act the Soul;   315
And one regards Itself, and one the Whole.
   Thus God and Nature linked the gen'ral frame,
And bade Self-love and Social be the same.

EPISTLE IV

ARGUMENT

OF THE NATURE AND STATE OF MAN, WITH RESPECT TO HAPPINESS

I. False notions of happiness, philosophical and popular, answered.
II. It is the end of all men, and attainable by all. God intends happiness to be equal; and to be so, it must be social, since all particular happiness depends on general, and since He governs by general, not particular laws. As it is necessary for order, and the peace and welfare of society, that external goods should be unequal, happiness is not made to consist in these. But, notwithstanding that inequality, the balance of happiness among mankind is kept even by Providence, by the two passions of hope and fear. III. What the happiness of individuals is, as far as is consistent with the constitution of this world; and that the good man has here the advantage. The error of imputing to virtue what are only the calamities of nature or of fortune. IV. The folly of expecting that God should alter his general laws in favour of particulars. V. That we are not judges who are good; but that whoever they are, they must be happiest. VI. That external goods are not the proper rewards, but often inconsistent with, or destructive of virtue. That even these can make no man happy without virtue: instanced in riches, honours, nobility, greatness, fame, superior talents. With pictures of human infelicity in men possessed of them all. VII. That virtue only constitutes a happiness, whose object is universal, and whose prospect eternal. That the perfection of virtue and happiness consists in a conformity to the order of Providence here, and a resignation to it here and hereafter.

OH HAPPINESS! our being's end and aim!
Good, Pleasure, Ease, Content! whate'er thy name:
That something still which prompts th' eternal sigh,
For which we bear to live, or dare to die,

Which still so near us, yet beyond us lies,   5
O'erlooked, seen double, by the fool, and wise.[1]
Plant of celestial seed! if dropped below,
Say, in what mortal soil thou deign'st to grow?
Fair op'ning to some Court's propitious shine,
Or deep with di'monds in the flaming mine?[2]   10
Twined with the wreaths Parnassian laurels yield,
Or reaped in iron harvests of the field?
Where grows?—where grows it not? If vain our toil,
We ought to blame the culture, not the soil:
Fixed to no spot is Happiness sincere,[3]   ·   15
'Tis nowhere to be found, or everywhere;
'Tis never to be bought, but always free,
And fled from Monarchs, St. John! dwells with thee.
    I.   Ask of the Learned the way? The Learned are blind:
This bids to serve, and that to shun mankind;   20
Some place the bliss in action, some in ease,
Those call it Pleasure, and Contentment these;
Some sunk to Beasts, find pleasure end in pain;
Some swelled to Gods, confess ev'n Virtue vain;
Or indolent, to each extreme they fall,   ·   25
To trust in everything, or doubt of all.[4]
    Who thus define it, say they more or less
Than this, that Happiness is Happiness?
    II.   Take Nature's path, and mad Opinion's leave;
All states can reach it, and all heads conceive;   30
Obvious her goods, in no extreme they dwell;

---

[1] "Overlooked in the things that would yield it, and in other things magnified by the imagination"—Elwin-Courthope.

[2] "Appropriate to the plant figure, on the old belief that minerals were organisms ripened by the sun's rays"—Mack. "Flaming" apparently means "emitting rays of light, flashing, glowing, brilliant"—*OED*.

[3] Genuine, pure, true.

[4] After once more contrasting the Stoics and Epicureans (ll. 20–24), Pope contrasts, according to Warburton, the Protagoreans, who believed "that every imagination or opinion of every man was true," to the Skeptics (ll. 25–26). The correctness of the Aristotelian mean is, of course, implied.

There needs but thinking right, and meaning well;
And mourn our various portions as we please,
Equal is Common Sense, and Common Ease.[5]
    Remember, Man, "the Universal Cause   35
"Acts not by partial, but by gen'ral laws";[6]
And makes what Happiness we justly call
Subsist not in the good of one, but all.
There's not a blessing Individuals find,
But some way leans and hearkens to the kind.[7]   40
No Bandit fierce, no Tyrant mad with pride,
No caverned Hermit, rests self-satisfied.
Who most to shun or hate Mankind pretend,
Seek an admirer, or would fix a friend.
Abstract what others feel, what others think,   45
All pleasures sicken, and all glories sink;
Each has his share; and who would more obtain,
Shall find, the pleasure pays not half the pain.
    ORDER is Heav'n's first law; and this confessed,
Some are, and must be, greater than the rest,   50
More rich, more wise; but who infers from hence
That such are happier, shocks all common sense.
Heav'n to Mankind impartial we confess,
If all are equal in their Happiness:
But mutual wants this Happiness increase;   55
All Nature's diff'rence keeps all Nature's peace.
Condition, circumstance is not the thing;
Bliss is the same in subject or in king,
In who obtain defence, or who defend,
In him who is, or him who finds a friend: 60
Heav'n breathes through every member of the whole
One common blessing, as one common soul.
But Fortune's gifts if each alike possessed,

---

5 Peace of mind.

  6 Cf. III. 1–2.

  7 "Man waits, as it were, all ear! for the approbation of another's feelings, before he can decide upon the reality of his own happiness from a
present enjoyment"—Wakefield.

And each were equal, must not all contest?[8]
If then to all Men Happiness was meant,   65
God in Externals could not place Content.

Fortune her gifts may variously dispose,
And these be happy called, unhappy those;
But Heav'n's just balance equal will appear,
While those are placed in Hope, and these in Fear: 70
Not present good or ill, the joy or curse,
But future views of better, or of worse.

Oh sons of earth! attempt ye still to rise,
By mountains piled on mountains, to the skies?
Heav'n still with laughter the vain toil surveys,   75
And buries madmen in the heaps they raise.[9]

III.   Know, all the good that individuals find,
Or God and Nature meant to mere Mankind,
Reason's whole pleasure, all the joys of Sense,
Lie in three words, Health, Peace, and Competence.[1]   80
But Health consists with Temperance alone,
And Peace, oh Virtue! Peace is all thy own.
The good or bad the gifts of Fortune gain,
But these less taste them, as they worse obtain.[2]
Say, in pursuit of profit or delight,   85
Who risk the most, that take wrong means, or right?
Of Vice or Virtue, whether blest or curst,
Which meets contempt, or which compassion first?
Count all th' advantage prosp'rous Vice attains,
'Tis but what Virtue flies from and disdains: 90
And grant the bad what happiness they would,

---

[8] A traditional argument for subordination.

[9] An allusion both to the attempt of the Titans to conquer Olympus by piling Ossa upon Pelion, and to the building of the tower of Babel. In *Paradise Lost*, God's response to Satan is derision and laughter (e.g., V. 735–737).

[1] "A sufficiency of means for living comfortably"—*OED*. Aristotle points out in the *Nicomachean Ethics* that even the virtuous man must have a "competence" to sustain life (1178a–1179a).

[2] To the extent they obtain them in a less admirable way.

One they must want,[3] which is, to pass for good.
  Oh blind to truth, and God's whole scheme below,
Who fancy Bliss to Vice, to Virtue Woe!
Who sees and follows that great scheme the best,   95
Best knows the blessing, and will most be blest.
But fools the Good alone unhappy call,
For ills or accidents that chance to all.
See FALKLAND dies, the virtuous and the just!
See godlike TURENNE prostrate on the dust!   100
See SIDNEY bleeds amid the martial strife![4]
Was this their Virtue, or Contempt of Life?[5]
Say, was it Virtue, more though Heav'n ne'er gave,
Lamented DIGBY! sunk thee to the grave?
Tell me, if Virtue made the Son expire,   105
Why, full of days and honour, lives the Sire?[6]
Why drew Marseille's good bishop purer breath,
When Nature sickened, and each gale was death?[7]
Or why so long (in life if long can be)
Lent Heav'n a parent to the poor and me?[8]   110
   IV.   What makes all physical or moral ill?
There deviates Nature, and here wanders Will.[9]
God sends not ill: if rightly understood,
Or partial Ill is universal Good,

---

[3] Lack.

[4] Lucius Cary, second Viscount Falkland, died fighting for Charles I in 1643; his friend Clarendon praised him highly in the *History of the Rebellion.* Henri de La Tour d'Auvergne, Vicomte de Turenne, the famous French marshal, was killed in 1675. Sir Philip Sidney made his celebrated exit at Zutphen in 1586.

[5] That is, they died because they experienced the "ills or accidents that chance to all," not because they were virtuous or despised life.

[6] Pope wrote an epitaph for the Hon. Robert Digby who died, aged forty, in 1726. Digby's father was still living when this Epistle was published.

[7] François de Belsunce de Castelmoron (1671–1755), notable for his charitable labors during the plague of 1720–1721.

[8] Pope's mother died in 1733 at the age of 91.

[9] See note on I. 150.

Or Change admits, or Nature lets it fall,   115
Short and but rare, till Man improved it all.[1]
We just as wisely might of Heav'n complain
That righteous Abel was destroyed by Cain,
As that the virtuous son is ill at ease
When his lewd father gave the dire disease.   120
Think we, like some weak Prince, th' Eternal Cause,
Prone for his fav'rites to reverse his laws?
   Shall burning Etna, if a sage requires,
Forget to thunder, and recall her fires?[2]
On air or sea new motions be impressed,   125
Oh blameless Bethel! to relieve thy breast?[3]
When the loose mountain trembles from on high,
Shall gravitation cease, if you go by?
Or some old temple, nodding to its fall,
For Chartres' head reserve the hanging wall?[4]   130
   V.   But still this world (so fitted for the knave)
Contents us not. A better shall we have?
A kingdom of the Just then let it be:
But first consider how those Just agree.
The good must merit God's peculiar care;   135
But who, but God, can tell us who they are?
One thinks on Calvin Heav'n's own spirit fell,
Another deems him instrument of hell;
If Calvin feel Heav'n's blessing, or its rod,
This cries there is, and that, there is no God.   140

---

1 Evil does not come from God. Either partial evil is universal good (as explained in I. 150 ff.), or results from change (mutability) inherent in the world, or was a transient and unusual aspect of Nature until man increased its amount by his corruption.

2 According to the most common story of his death, the philosopher Empedocles "to be deemed / A God, leaped fondly into Etna flames"— *Paradise Lost* III. 469–470. Another account states that Empedocles perished when he approached too near the volcano while investigating its eruptions.

3 Hugh Bethel, a sufferer from asthma, to whom Pope addressed his *Second Satire of the Second Book of Horace.*

4 Francis Chartres (pronounced *Charters*) was a notorious contemporary villain.

What shocks one part will edify the rest,
Nor with one system can they all be blest.
The very best will variously incline,
And what rewards your Virtue, punish mine.
"WHATEVER IS, IS RIGHT."—This world, 'tis true,   145
Was made for Caesar—but for Titus too:
And which more blest? who chained his country,[5] say,
Or he whose Virtue sighed to lose a day?[6]
   "But sometimes Virtue starves, while Vice is fed."
What then? Is the reward of Virtue bread?   150
That, Vice may merit; 'tis the price of toil;
The knave deserves it, when he tills the soil,
The knave deserves it, when he tempts[7] the main,
Where Folly fights for kings, or dives for gain.
The good man may be weak, be indolent,   155
Nor is his claim to plenty, but content.
But grant him Riches, your demand is o'er?
"No—shall the good want Health, the good want Pow'r?"
Add Health, and Pow'r, and every earthly thing;
"Why bounded Pow'r? why private? why no king?"   160
Nay, why external for internal giv'n?
Why is not Man a God, and Earth a Heav'n?
Who ask and reason thus will scarce conceive
God gives enough, while he has more to give:
Immense the pow'r, immense were the demand;   165
Say, at what part of nature will they stand?
   VI.   What nothing earthly gives, or can destroy,
The soul's calm sunshine, and the heartfelt joy,
Is Virtue's prize: A better would you fix?
Then give Humility a coach and six,   170
Justice a Conq'ror's sword, or Truth a gown,[8]
Or Public Spirit its great cure, a Crown.

---

[5] Caesar.

[6] So Suetonius reports of Titus.

[7] Attempts, hazards himself on.

[8] "This may refer to the gown of a University degree, or, as in 197, to the preacher's gown"—Morris.

Weak, foolish man! will Heav'n reward us there
With the same trash mad mortals wish for here?
The Boy and Man an individual makes,   175
Yet sigh'st thou now for apples and for cakes?
Go, like the Indian, in another life
Expect thy dog, thy bottle, and thy wife:[9]
As well as dream such trifles are assigned,
As toys and empires, for a godlike mind.   180
Rewards, that either would to Virtue bring
No joy, or be destructive of the thing:
How oft by these at sixty are undone
The virtues of a saint at twenty-one!

   To whom can Riches give Repute, or Trust,   185
Content, or Pleasure, but the Good and Just?
Judges and Senates have been bought for gold,
Esteem and Love were never to be sold.
Oh fool! to think God hates the worthy mind,
The lover and the love of humankind,   190
Whose life is healthful, and whose conscience clear,
Because he wants a thousand pounds a year.

   Honour and shame from no Condition rise;
Act well your part, there all the honour lies.
Fortune in Men has some small diff'rence made,   195
One flaunts in rags, one flutters in brocade,
The cobbler aproned, and the parson gowned,
The friar hooded, and the monarch crowned.
"What differ more (you cry) than crown and cowl?"
I'll tell you, friend! a Wise man and a Fool.[1]   200
You'll find, if once the monarch acts the monk,
Or, cobbler-like, the parson will be drunk,
Worth makes the man, and want of it, the fellow;[2]
The rest is all but leather or prunella.[3]

---

   [9] See I. 99–112.
   [1] Possibly sometimes pronounced *fowl*.
   [2] Pronounced, as it often still is, *fel-la* and meaning a worthless person.
   [3] The cobbler's leather apron and the parson's prunella (twilled woolen) gown.

Stuck o'er with titles and hung round with strings,[4]   205
That thou mayst be by kings, or whores of kings.
Boast the pure blood of an illustrious race,
In quiet flow from Lucrece to Lucrece;[5]
But by your father's worth if yours you rate,
Count me those only who were good and great.   210
Go! if your ancient, but ignoble blood
Has crept through scoundrels ever since the flood,
Go! and pretend your family is young;
Nor own, your fathers have been fools so long.
What can ennoble sots, or slaves, or cowards?   215
Alas! not all the blood of all the HOWARDS.[6]
   Look next on Greatness; say where Greatness lies?
"Where, but among the Heroes and the Wise?"
Heroes are much the same, the point's agreed,
From Macedonia's madman to the Swede;[7]   220
The whole strange purpose of their lives, to find
Or make, an enemy of all mankind!
Not one looks backward, onward still he goes,
Yet ne'er looks forward farther than his nose.
No less alike the Politic and Wise,   225
All sly slow things, with circumspective eyes:
Men in their loose unguarded hours they take,
Not that themselves are wise, but others weak.
But grant that those can conquer, these can cheat,
'Tis phrase absurd to call a Villain Great: 230
Who wickedly is wise, or madly brave,
Is but the more a fool, the more a knave.
Who noble ends by noble means obtains,
Or failing, smiles in exile or in chains,

---

4 Decorations.
  5 The Roman matron who killed herself for shame after being raped.
  6 The family headed by the Duke of Norfolk, the premier duke, premier earl, and hereditary Earl Marshal of England.
  7 From Alexander the Great to Charles XII of Sweden (r. 1697–1718), who was called "The Alexander of the North."

Like good Aurelius[8] let him reign, or bleed   235
Like Socrates, that Man is great indeed.
   What's Fame? a fancied life in others' breath,
A thing beyond us, ev'n before our death.
Just what you hear, you have, and what's unknown
The same (my Lord)[9] if Tully's, or your own.   240
All that we feel of it begins and ends
In the small circle of our foes or friends;
To all beside as much as empty shade
An Eugene[1] living, as a Caesar dead;
Alike or when, or where, they shone, or shine,   245
Or on the Rubicon, or on the Rhine.
A Wit's a feather, and a Chief a rod;[2]
An honest[3] Man's the noblest work of God.
Fame but from death a villain's name can save,
As Justice tears his body from the grave,   250
When what t' oblivion better were resigned,
Is hung on high, to poison half mankind.[4]
All fame is foreign, but of true desert;[5]
Plays round the head, but comes not to the heart:
One self-approving hour whole years outweighs   255
Of stupid starers, and of loud huzzas;[6]
And more true joy Marcellus[7] exiled feels,

---

   [8] Marcus Aurelius Antoninus, Roman emperor (r. 161–180) and Stoic
philosopher.

   [9] Bolingbroke, whose abilities, reputation, and perhaps career, are being
implicitly compared to Marcus Tullius Cicero's.

   [1] The famous Austrian general, Prince Eugene of Savoy (1663–1736), who
campaigned on the Rhine (IV. 246) against the French in 1734.

   [2] "Alluding to the pen with which the wit writes, and the baton or
truncheon . . . of the general"—Pattison.

   [3] About equivalent to "good" or "virtuous." As Empson says of this
couplet, "all the faults suggested in *wit* and *chief* are opposed to virtues
that *honest* could be used to praise."

   [4] Perhaps a reference to the hanging of the corpses of Charles I's judges
on the gallows at the Restoration.

   [5] But what is truly deserved. "Desert" is pronounced *des-art'*.

   [6] Pronounced to rhyme with "outweighs."

   [7] Marcus Claudius Marcellus, died 46 B.C., an enemy of Caesar.

Than Caesar with a senate at his heels.
　In Parts[8] superior what advantage lies?
Tell (for You[9] can) what is it to be wise?　　　　260
'Tis but to know how little can be known;
To see all others' faults, and feel our own:
Condemned in business or in arts to drudge
Without a second,[1] or without a judge:
Truths would you teach, or save a sinking land?　265
All fear, none aid you, and few understand.
Painful preheminence! yourself to view
Above life's weakness, and its comforts too.
　Bring then these blessings to a strict account,
Make fair deductions, see to what they mount.　270
How much of other each is sure to cost;
How each for other oft is wholly lost;
How inconsistent greater goods with these;
How sometimes life is risked, and always ease:
Think, and if still the things thy envy call,[2]　275
Say, wouldst thou be the Man to whom they fall?
To sigh for ribbands[3] if thou art so silly,
Mark how they grace Lord Umbra, or Sir Billy:
Is yellow dirt the passion of thy life?
Look but on Gripus, or on Gripus' wife:　　　　280
If Parts allure thee, think how Bacon shined,
The wisest, brightest, meanest of mankind:
Or ravished with the whistling of a Name,
See Cromwell, damned to everlasting fame!
If all,[4] united, thy ambition call,　　　　　　285
From ancient story learn to scorn them all.
There, in the rich, the honoured, famed, and great,
See the false scale[5] of Happiness complete!

---

8 Natural abilities.
9 Bolingbroke.
1 Supporter.
2 Call forth.
3 Ribbons, decorations.
4 Honors, money, etc.
5 Hierarchy.

In hearts of Kings, or arms of Queens who lay,
How happy! those to ruin, these betray.[6]   290
Mark by what wretched steps their glory grows,
From dirt and seaweed as proud Venice rose;
In each how guilt and greatness equal ran,
And all that raised the Hero, sunk the Man.
Now Europe's laurels on their brows behold,   295
But stained with blood, or ill exchanged for gold;
Then see them broke with toils, or sunk in ease,
Or infamous for plundered provinces.
Oh wealth ill-fated! which no act of fame
E'er taught to shine, or sanctified from shame!   300
What greater bliss attends their close of life?
Some greedy minion, or imperious wife,
The trophied arches, storied halls invade,
And haunt their slumbers in the pompous shade.
Alas! not dazzled with their noontide ray,   305
Compute the morn and evening to the day;
The whole amount of that enormous fame,
A Tale, that blends their glory with their shame!
    VII.   Know then this truth (enough for Man to know)
"Virtue alone is Happiness below."   310
The only point where human bliss stands still,
And tastes the good without the fall to ill;
Where only Merit[7] constant pay receives,
Is blest in what it takes, and what it gives;[8]
The joy unequalled, if its end it gain,   315
And if it lose, attended with no pain:
Without satiety, though e'er so blessed;
And but more relished as the more distressed:[9]

---

[6] "What a form their happiness took, consisting in ruining the kings who trusted and the queens who loved them"—Thompson.

[7] The only point where merit. . . .

[8] It is blessed to receive as well as give. Virtue here assumes its active form of benevolence.

[9] Virtue is only the more prized if it is harassed, disappointed, or despised.

The broadest mirth unfeeling Folly wears,
Less pleasing far than Virtue's very tears.   320
Good, from each object, from each place acquired,
For ever exercised, yet never tired;
Never elated, while one man's oppressed;
Never dejected, while another's blessed;
And where no wants, no wishes can remain,   325
Since but to wish more Virtue, is to gain.
   See! the sole bliss Heav'n could on all bestow;
Which who but feels can taste, but thinks can know:
Yet poor with fortune, and with learning blind,
The bad must miss; the good, untaught, will find;   330
Slave to no sect, who takes no private road,
But looks through Nature up to Nature's God;
Pursues that Chain which links th' immense design,
Joins heav'n and earth, and mortal and divine;
Sees, that no Being any bliss can know,   335
But touches some above, and some below;
Learns, from this union of the rising Whole,
The first, last purpose of the human soul;
And knows where Faith, Law, Morals, all began,
All end, in LOVE OF GOD, and LOVE OF MAN.   340
   For him alone, Hope leads from goal to goal,
And opens still, and opens on his soul;[1]
Till lengthened on to Faith, and unconfined,
It pours the bliss that fills up all the mind.
He sees, why Nature plants in Man alone   345
Hope of known bliss, and Faith in bliss unknown:
(Nature, whose dictates to no other kind
Are giv'n in vain, but what they seek they find)
Wise is her present; she connects in this
His greatest Virtue with his greatest Bliss: 350
At once his own bright prospect to be blest,
And strongest motive to assist the rest.
   Self-love thus pushed to social, to divine,

---

1 And opens always (on new goals) and finally gives hope for his soul's
salvation.

Gives thee to make thy neighbour's blessing thine.
Is this too little for the boundless heart?   355
Extend it, let thy enemies have part:
Grasp the whole worlds of Reason, Life, and Sense,[2]
In one close system of Benevolence:
Happier as kinder, in whate'er degree,
And height of Bliss but height of Charity.   360
    God loves from Whole to Parts: But human soul
Must rise from Individual to the Whole.
Self-love but serves the virtuous mind to wake,
As the small pebble stirs the peaceful lake;
The centre moved, a circle strait[3] succeeds,   365
Another still, and still another spreads,
Friend, parent, neighbour, first it will embrace,
His country next, and next all human race,
Wide and more wide, th' o'erflowings of the mind
Take every creature in, of every kind;   370
Earth smiles around, with boundless bounty blest,
And Heav'n beholds its image in his breast.
    Come then, my Friend, my Genius,[4] come along,
Oh master of the poet, and the song!
And while the Muse now stoops, or now ascends,   375
To Man's low passions, or their glorious ends,
Teach me, like thee, in various nature wise,
To fall with dignity, with temper rise;
Formed by thy converse, happily to steer
From grave to gay, from lively to severe;   380
Correct with spirit, eloquent with ease,
Intent to reason, or polite to please.
Oh! while along the stream of Time thy name
Expanded flies, and gathers all its fame,
Say, shall my little bark attendant sail,   385
Pursue the triumph, and partake the gale?
When statesmen, heroes, kings, in dust repose,

---

[2] The worlds containing life, feeling (sense, as in animals), and reason.
[3] (1) Straightway; (2) narrow (?).
[4] Bolingbroke, as guiding spirit.

Whose sons shall blush their fathers were thy foes,
Shall then this verse to future age pretend[5]
Thou wert my guide, philosopher, and friend?   390
That urged by thee, I turned the tuneful art
From sounds to things, from fancy to the heart;
For Wit's false mirror held up Nature's light;
Showed erring Pride, WHATEVER IS, IS RIGHT;
That REASON, PASSION, answer one great aim;   395
That true SELF-LOVE and SOCIAL are the same;
That VIRTUE only makes our Bliss below;
And all our Knowledge is, OURSELVES TO KNOW.

---

5 Assert.